S0-FBE-230

TEN KEYS to Good Manners

Ten Keys Series idea from Claire Boutrolle d'Estaimbuc

Under the direction of Romain Lizé, President, MAGNIFICAT
Editor, MAGNIFICAT: Isabelle Galmiche
Editors, Ignatius: Vivian Dudro and Catherine Harmon
Translator: MAGNIFICAT - Ignatius
Proofreader: Kathleen Hollenbeck
Layout: Magali Meunier
Production: Thierry Dubus, Audrey Bord

Original French édition: *Les 10 clefs des bonnes manières*
© 2020, Pierre Téqui éditeur, Paris, France

© 2025 by MAGNIFICAT, New York • Ignatius Press, San Francisco
All rights reserved
ISBN MAGNIFICAT 978-1-63967-107-6 • ISBN Ignatius Press 978-1-62164-757-7

Claire Boutrolle d'Estaimbuc & By•bm
Foreword by Kendra Tierney

TEN KEYS
to Good
Manners

MAGNIFICAT • Ignatius

To my three daughters

CONTENTS

Foreword 6

The First Key
★ The Five Magic Words 8

The Second Key
★ Body Language 10

The Third Key
★ Punctuality 12

The Fourth Key
★ Respecting Your Elders 14

The Fifth Key
★ Table Manners 16

The Sixth Key
★ Using the Right Words at the Right Time 18

The Seventh Key
★ Being a Good Guest 20

The Eighth Key
★ Receiving Gifts Graciously 22

The Ninth Key
★ Accepting Compliments 24

The Tenth Key
★ Thinking of Others 26

Setting and Using Tableware 28
It's Your Turn! 30
Conclusion 31
Good Job! 32

Dear Children,

Hi! I'm very glad that someone has given you this book. Clearly, whoever it was cares about you and wants the best for you!

This book was written by a mother, with love, for her own children. I'm also a mom, and I'm grateful to be able to share it with my kids. Parents have a lot of responsibilities, and one of them is to help their children become the kind of people that others like to be around.

At first, good manners can feel like a bunch of silly rules. But, really, good manners are an age-old secret to feeling more comfortable around other people. Once we understand them, and they come from the heart, good manners help us love the people around us in genuine, practical ways. Such kindness and care for others makes us lovable... and loved.

Using good manners is an easy way to begin our exercise of Christian virtues. They help us put the comfort and feelings of others over our own. The more we do this, the easier it becomes.

Read this charming little book and see how simple using good manners can be!

Sincerely,

Kendra Tierney Norton, Author
Catholic All Year Compendium:
Liturgical Living for Real Life

P.S.: Quick, turn to page 22 and be sure to give a proper thank-you to the person who gave you this book!

THE FIRST KEY

★ The Five Magic Words ★

The first and most important key to showing respect and love for others is very simple: use the magic words! There are five of these phrases; can you guess what they are?

P . . . .   T . . . .   y . .

Y . ' . .   w . . . .

E . . . .   m .   I ' .   s . . . .

TIP

Include the name of the person to whom you're speaking when you use the magic words; you may also use "ma'am" or "sir" when speaking to an adult. For example, "Thank you, Mom"; "You're welcome, Jack"; "I'm sorry, ma'am"; "Excuse me, sir."

Answers:
Please; thank you; you're welcome; excuse me; I'm sorry

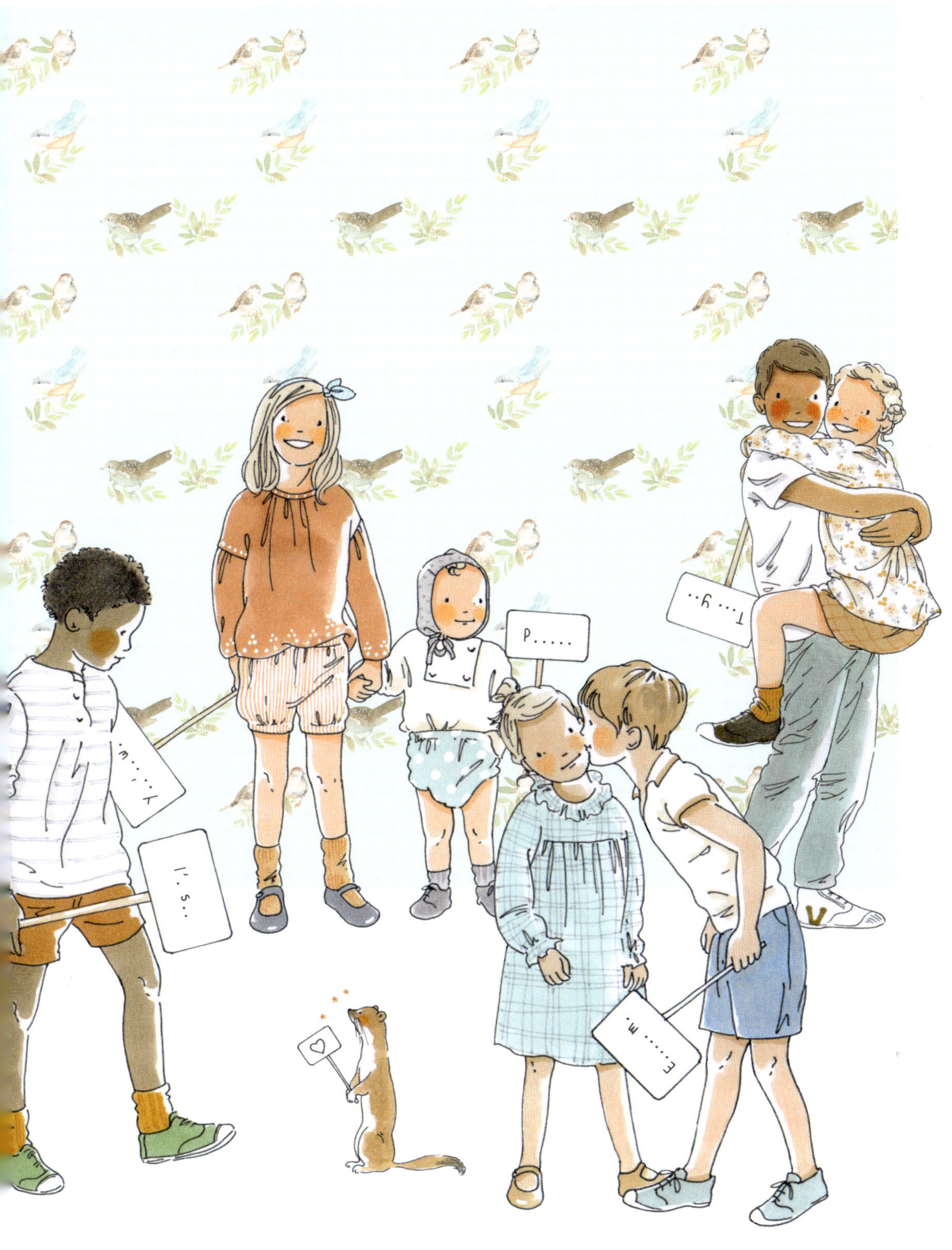
P.....

The Second Key

Body Language

Stand up straight, and face forward. Don't drag your feet when you walk, and keep your hands out of your pockets. Smile when you're in a good mood; you will find that joy is contagious!

When someone talks to you, make eye contact when answering. Avoid chewing gum during a conversation.

When shaking hands, offer a firm handshake. This shows confidence and inspires trust. This key, like all the others in this book, will be very helpful when you grow up too!

When you're in a line, wait patiently for your turn. Sit still without fidgeting or slouching if you are seated.

TIP

Put your hand over your mouth when you yawn. Of course, no fingers in your nose! Blow your nose with a tissue, as discreetly as you can. When you sneeze, laugh, or speak in a public place, try not to draw attention to yourself by being too loud.

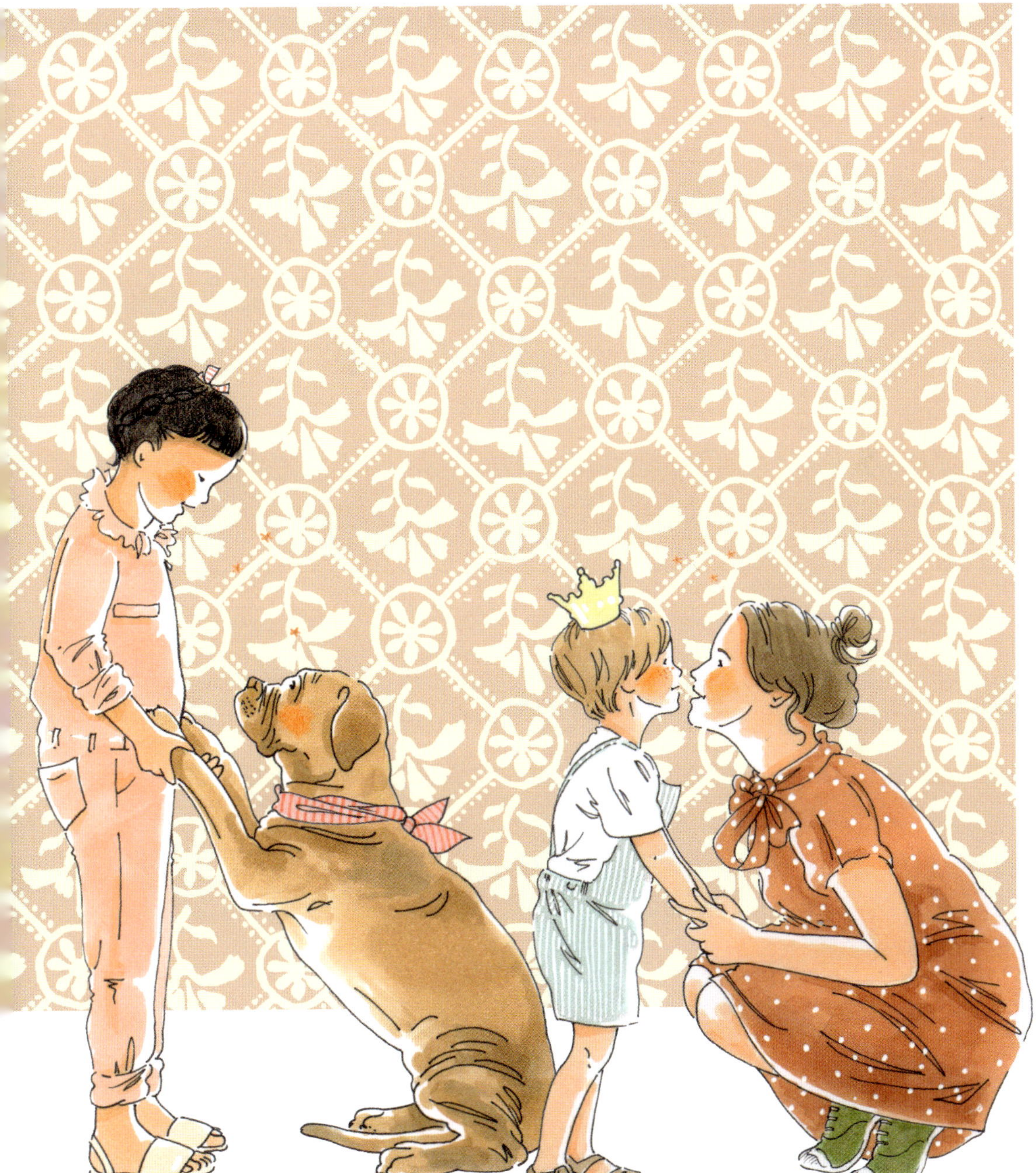

The Third Key

Punctuality

Always do your best to be on time. It is a sign of respect for others that everyone should observe. By being punctual and not keeping others waiting, you show them that you value their time and that they are important to you.

"Punctuality is the courtesy of kings." This phrase, attributed to King Louis XVIII of France, applies to anyone, at any age.

TIP

When you are grown-up and invited for dinner or lunch at someone's home, it isn't considered rude to arrive a few minutes late, but arriving early, when not expressly asked to, is rude since your host might not be ready.
When going to the airport and the doctor's or the dentist's office, however, it is better to be early!

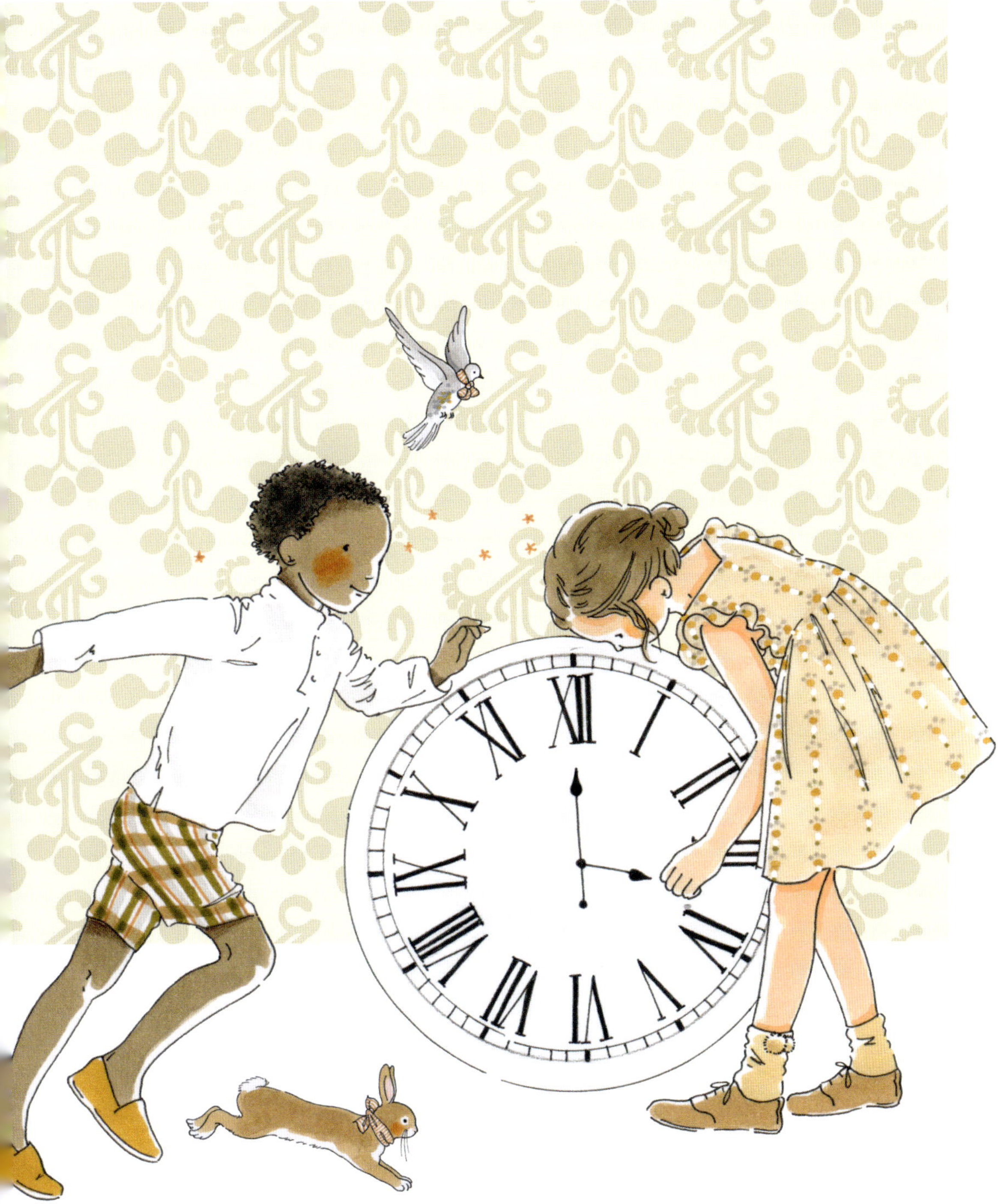

The Fourth Key

Respecting Your Elders

You should show respect toward everyone, especially toward adults, and in particular toward your parents. Being polite and cooperative with your parents shows them that you are thankful for their loving care. Being respectful to other adults reflects well on your family and prepares you for being an adult yourself.

If you are seated, and an adult comes in, get up to offer him or her your seat. Often, the person will decline and tell you to remain seated, but your show of respect is still appreciated.

When dining with your parents or other adults, ask permission to be excused from the table when you have finished eating.

In the past, children were only allowed to speak at the table when spoken to by an adult. Rules about this have changed and eased over time. But you should not interrupt conversations or cut people off, and never correct adults in front of others. If you think they are saying something wrong, wait until later to talk about it with your parents in private.

TIP

When having a conversation with adults, be careful not to show off or talk more than everyone else.

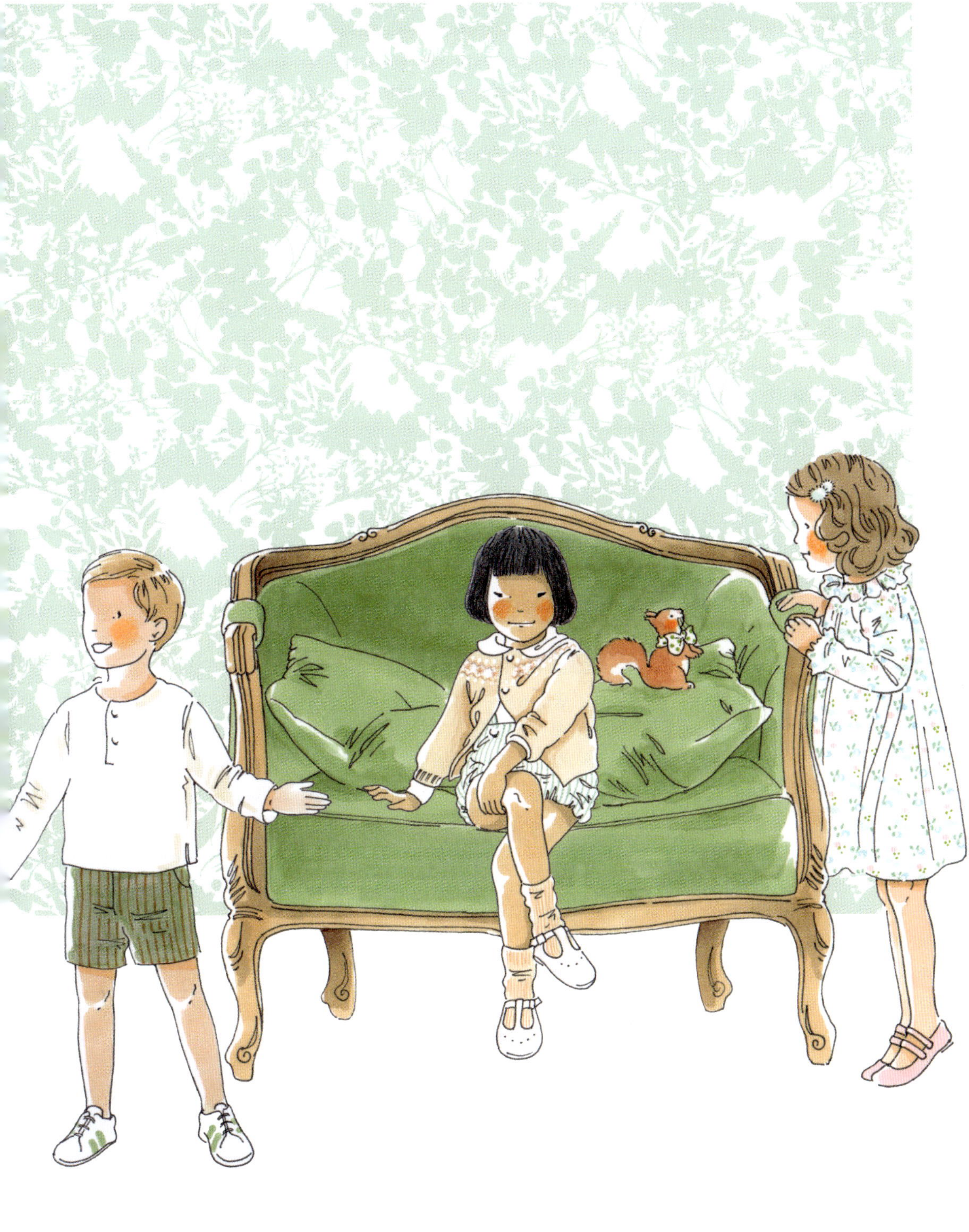

THE FIFTH KEY

★ Table Manners ★

The fifth key is very important when you are at home with your family, in the home of others, or at a restaurant: table manners!

Sit up straight, and keep your mouth closed while chewing—no one wants to see inside your mouth, besides the dentist!

Keep your elbows off the table, and hold them close to your body when lifting a spoon or a fork to your mouth to avoid bumping into your neighbors. When not using your hands to eat, keep them in your lap.

Do not talk with your mouth full. Do not chew noisily while eating or make slurping noises while drinking.

Cut small bites of food, and do not put too much food into your mouth at once.

When done eating, put your silverware on top of your plate, which will be helpful for the person clearing the table.

Finally, wait to leave the table until everyone has finished eating, and always ask to be excused.

TIP

Sit closer to the table than to the back of your chair to avoid spills and drips. Remember to use your magic words—please, thank you— when you need something on the table, instead of reaching out and grabbing it yourself.

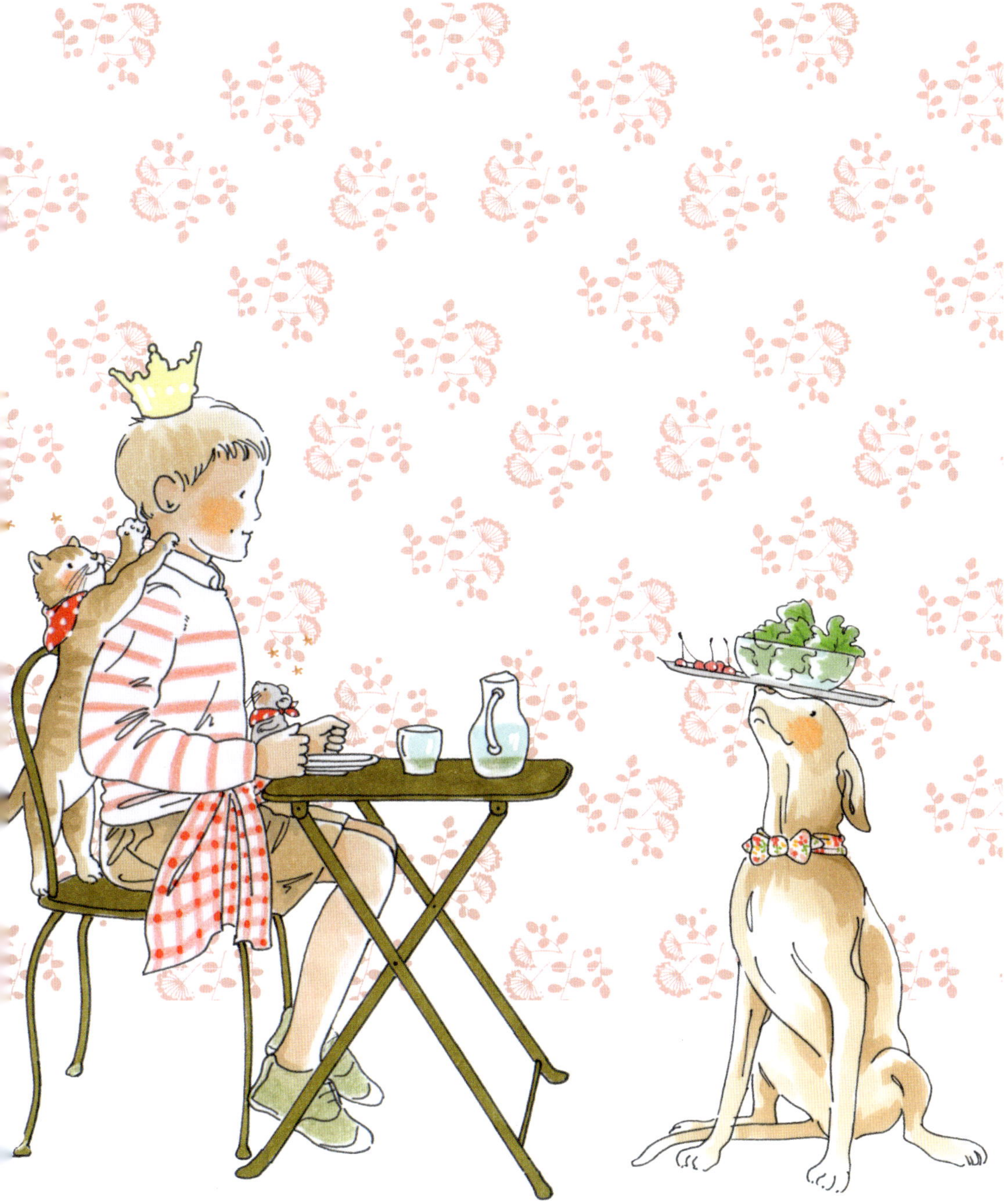

The Sixth Key

Using the Right Words at the Right Time

To the best of your ability, use correct grammar. To ask for permission, say "May I … ?" not "Can I … ?" When you are the subject of the verb, use "I"; if the object, use "me": "Luke and I are going outside"; "Anna invited Maggie and me to her party."

Avoid using slang in formal situations, or when speaking with your teachers or other adults in authority. Say "Yes" not "Yeah"; "No" not "Nah"; "No thank you" not "I'm good"; "I don't mind either way" not "Whatever!" When you need someone to repeat what he or she said, try "Pardon?" instead of "What?"

Do not use crude words or discuss in public things that should remain private. You should not make jokes about bodily functions or private parts.

Never take the Lord's name in vain or joke about holy things.

TIP

It can be difficult to know the right words to say, especially if you are angry or upset. If you can, wait until you are calmer to speak. If you have said something rude or mean to someone, apologize and resolve to do better next time.

Jack invited me to his house.
May I go, please?

The Seventh Key

★ Being a Good Guest ★

When you are invited over to a friend's house, it is very important to behave nicely and use your best manners. Here are a few reminders to help you and your host enjoy your visit:
- Offer to help without waiting to be asked.
- If you're staying overnight, make your bed and tidy your belongings.
- Do not reject the food you are served, even if it isn't your favorite thing to eat. If it is something you've never tried before, you may find that you like it! Unless it contains something you're allergic to, you should politely accept any food that is offered to you.
- When you leave, thank your hosts for their hospitality and for the good time you had with them.

TIP

Once back home, send your host a thank-you note; it can be a simple text message or a handwritten letter or card.

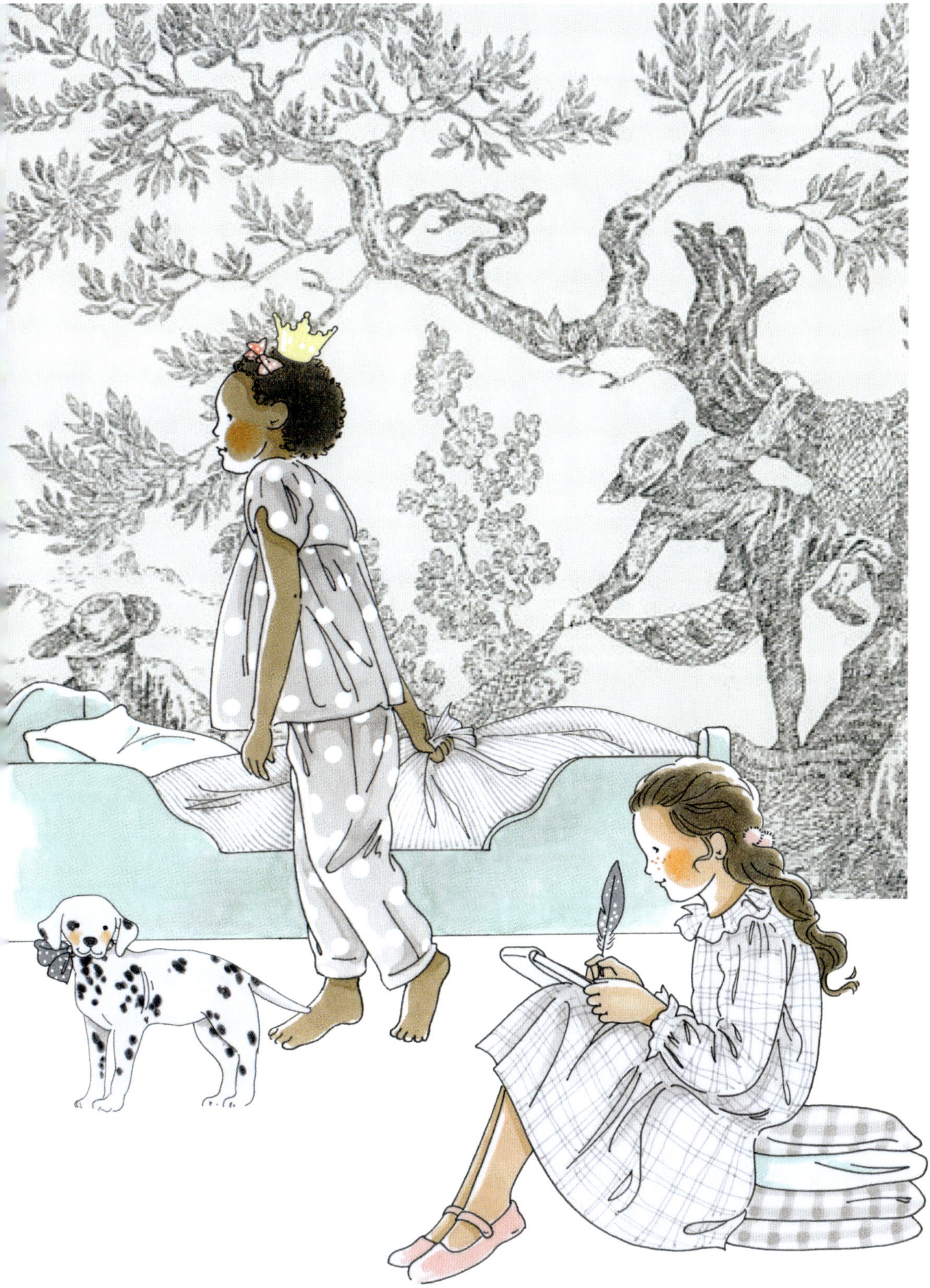

The Eighth Key

Receiving Gifts Graciously

It is always exciting to receive a gift! You should say "thank you" promptly, either in person or with a note or call, whenever someone gives you a gift.

What if you are given a gift, and you already have the exact same game, book, or toy? You should not mention this to the gift-giver; if your parents think the person should know, they will tell him or her. Say "thank you" for the gift, and for the giver's generosity.

TIP

When you write a thank-you note or call to say "thank you" for a gift, say how much you appreciate the gift-giver's thoughtfulness or kindness. If you can, say how much the gift means to you or how you are using or plan to use it.

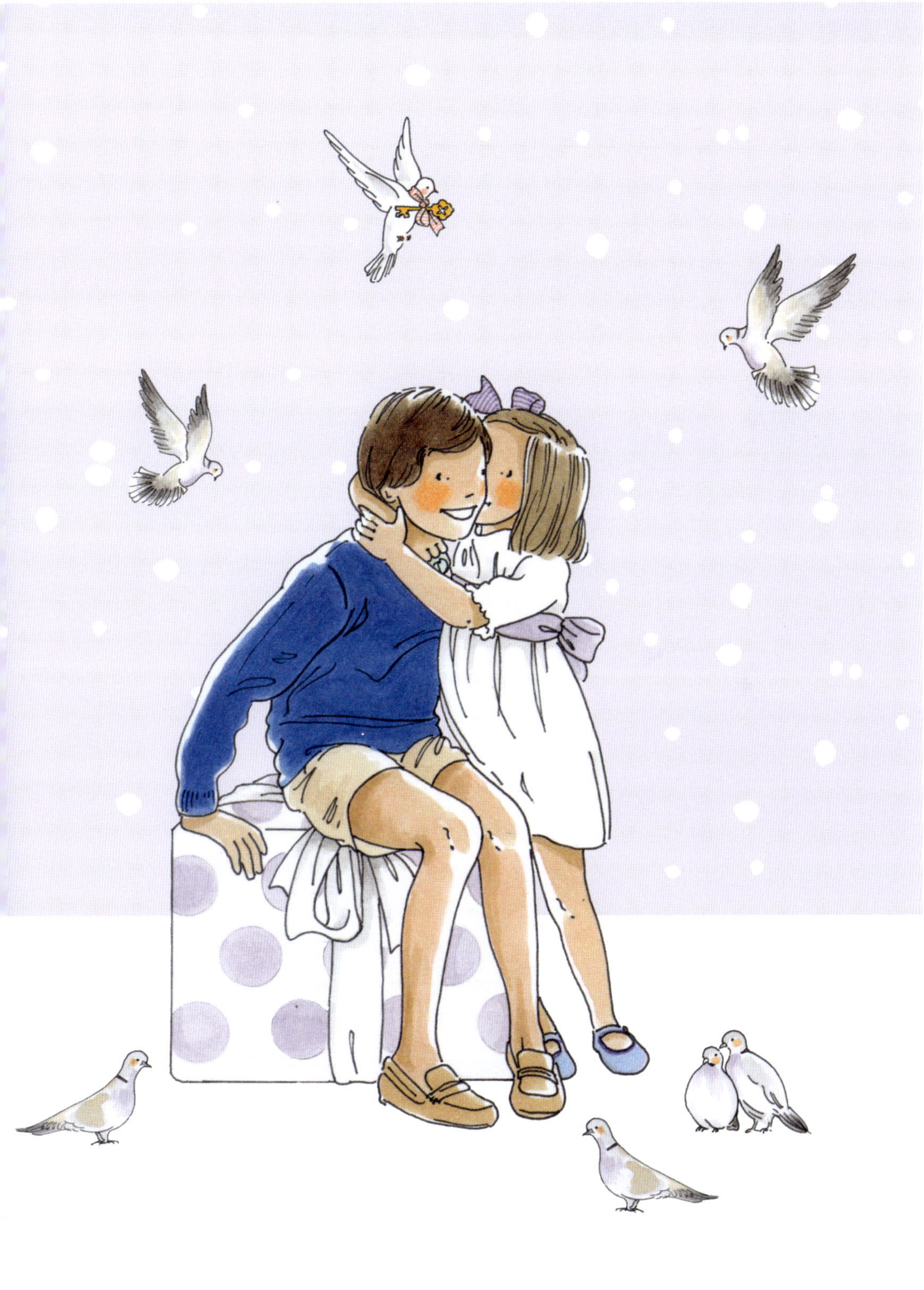

The Ninth Key

Accepting Compliments

Isn't it nice to receive a compliment? It can feel wonderful when someone praises you or something you've done. But sometimes you may feel a little embarrassed, or not know how to respond. It is simple: always say with a smile—Thank you!

TIP

If someone compliments you on an accomplishment involving others, it's important to include them. For example, if you are praised for winning a soccer game, say, "Thank you! Our team played hard together. We couldn't have done it alone!" This way, you recognize the merit of others, and share the glory with them.

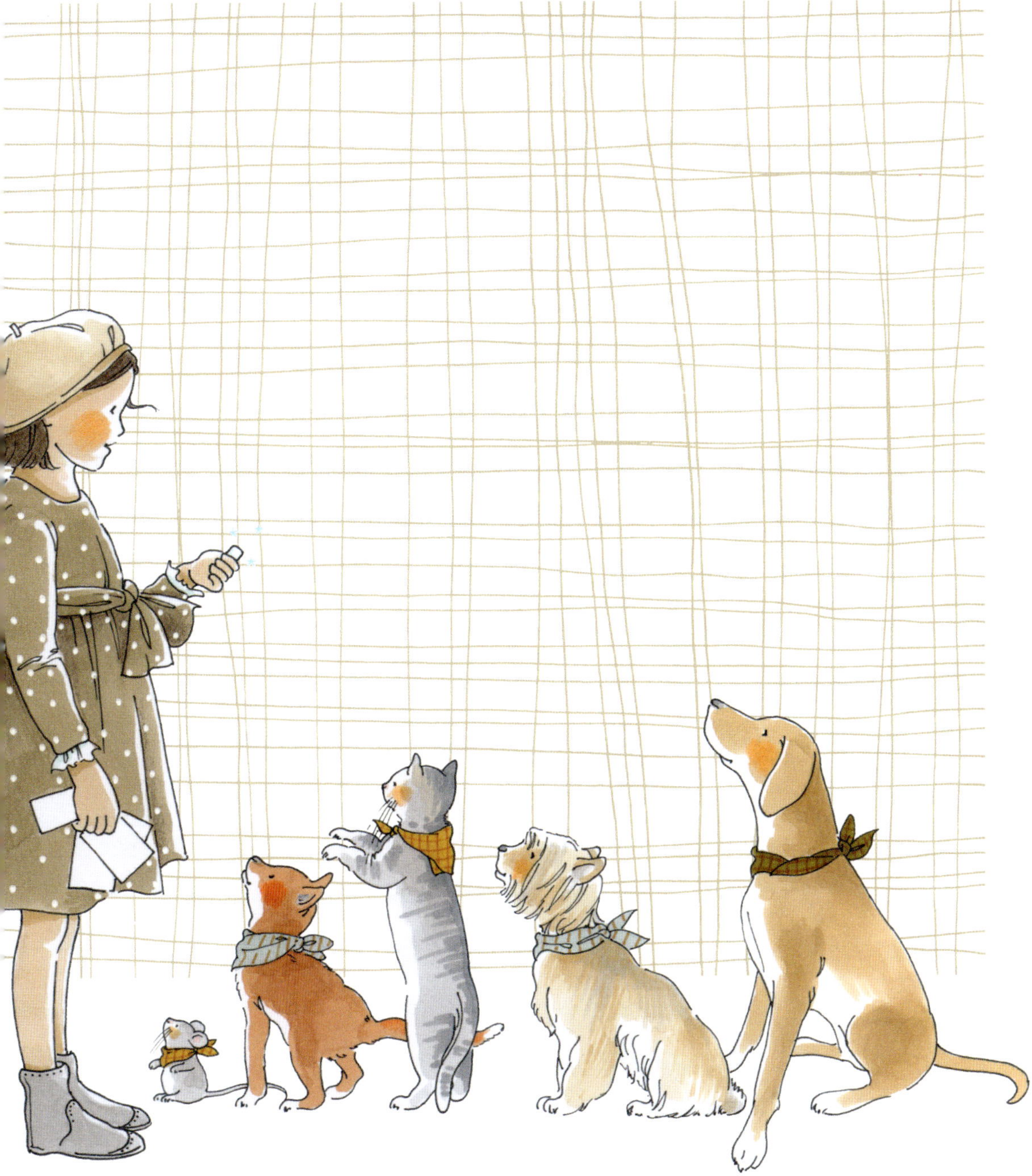

The Tenth Key

Thinking of Others

$\mathcal{B}$e considerate of others and their feelings in your words and actions. If you lose a game, do not be angry or resentful—take this opportunity to learn from your mistakes and do better next time. If you win, do not brag or put others down—show respect for your opponents and be considerate of their feelings.

Treat everyone with respect, and be especially kind to those who are smaller or less fortunate than you. Never make fun of others for their weaknesses or their differences.

If you hurt someone's feelings, on purpose or by accident, be sure to say that you are sorry. Also apologize if you lose or break something that belongs to another. Offer to fix or replace it. Always return in good condition whatever you borrow.

TIP

The Golden Rule is simple: "Treat others as you wish to be treated."

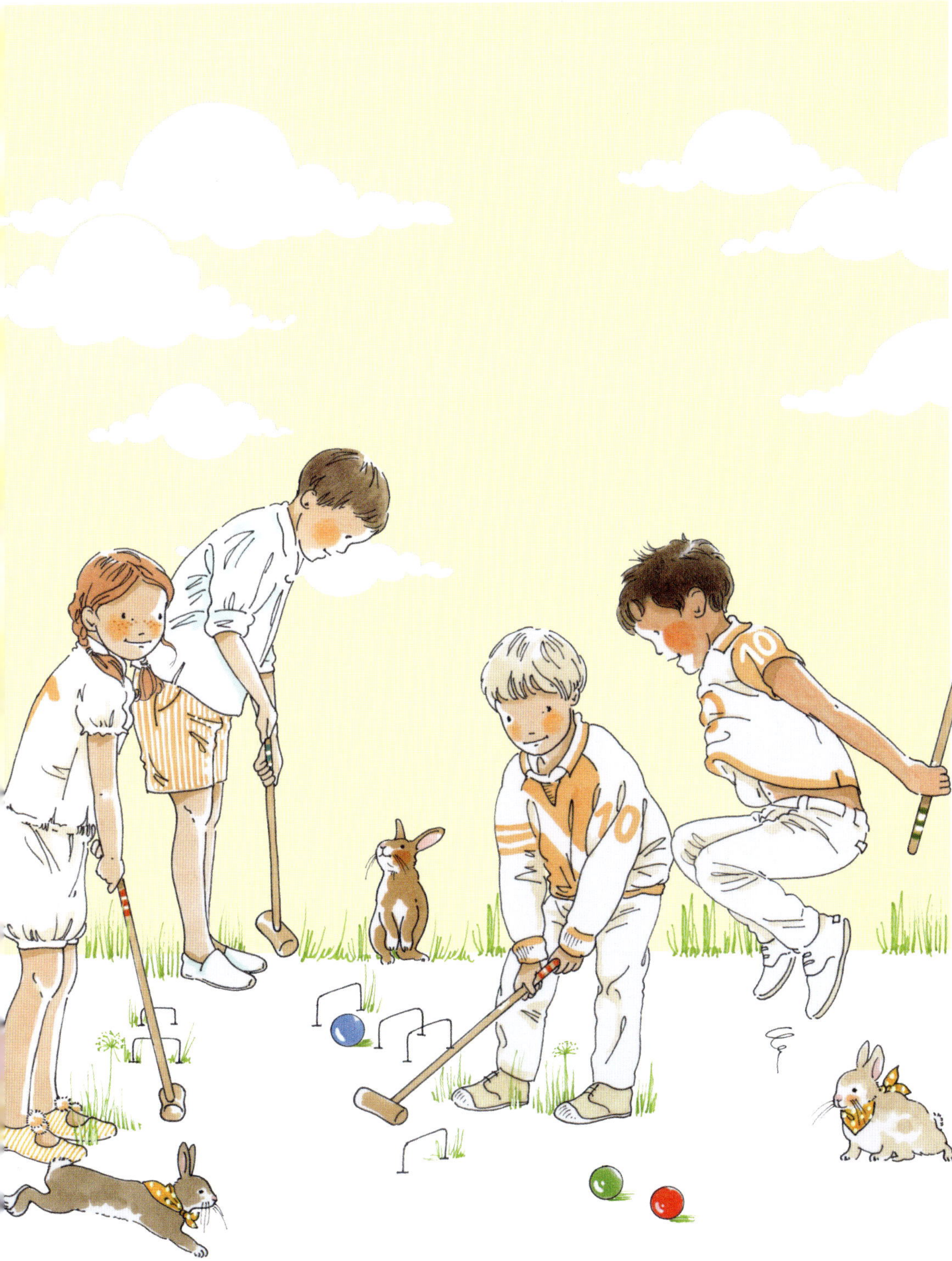

★ Setting and Using Tableware ★

$\mathcal{D}$o you know where to put your fork, spoon, and knife when setting the table for an everyday meal or a fancy dinner?

- Your fork should be to the left of your plate, tines facing up.

- Your knife should be to the right of your plate, with the blade facing the plate.

- Your napkin could be put to the left of your fork or on top of your plate.

For a more formal meal, you may have several forks, knives, and spoons. Use the ones furthest from the plate first. These could include a soup spoon on the right, a salad or side fork on the left, and a knife for cutting a side dish on the right. Dessert forks and/or spoons are set above the plate, with fork prongs facing right and spoons facing left. A butter knife can be set at an angle on top of a bread plate set to the left, above the forks. Glassware goes on the right.

In the United States, hold your knife in your right hand to cut a bite. Once you've finished cutting, place the knife on the plate and move the fork to your right hand. This way, you aren't holding a knife while eating. When you are done eating, place the fork and knife next to each other on your plate.

GOOD TO KNOW

Tables are set for right-handed people because most people are right-handed. In the past, left-handed people were expected to use their utensils as if they were right-handed. In recent years, more accommodations have been made for left-handed people, and in many places it is not considered bad manners for them to use knives and forks with their left hands.

★ It's Your Turn! ★

*T*ake the quiz below and see how good your manners are!
Correct answers can be found on page 32.

1. You break something by mistake; what do you do?
- ○ You lie: "I didn't do it; the cat did!"
- ○ You run away.
- ○ You apologize.
- ○ You laugh; who cares?

2. You are seated at the table; what do you do?
Correct the bad manners on the left with the good manners on the right!

You are slumped over the table.	You chew with your mouth closed.
You eat with your fingers.	You wipe your mouth and hands with your napkin.
You talk with your mouth full.	You put your napkin on your knees.
You put your napkin on your head.	You use your fork, spoon, and knife to eat.
You wipe your hands on your pants.	You sit up straight.

★ Conclusion ★

The rules about good manners can change over time or be different in other places and cultures. But showing respect is always important no matter where we are. Using good manners is a way to show people that we care about them. When we treat family members, friends, teachers, and people we come across at the store or the park with respect, we are treating them as children of God—just as we would like to be treated!

Mastering good manners as a child will help you grow into a polite and considerate adult—the kind of person who makes a great friend, parent, and coworker. A person who follows and leads others to Jesus!

As you practice good manners, don't be afraid to show your personality; a sense of humor, imagination, and creativity are even more appreciated in someone who is also polite and kind.

*You can feel confident and at ease
in all circumstances,
because good manners
give you the keys
to open any doors,
especially the doors to the hearts of others.*

★ Good Job! ★

You're a *Good Manners Hero*. Here is your crown!

1. You break something by mistake; what do you do?
- ○ You lie: "I didn't do it; the cat did!"
- ○ You run away.
- ✓ **You apologize.**
- ○ You laugh; who cares?

2. You are seated at the table; what do you do?
Correct the bad manners on the left with the good manners on the right!

Bad manners	Good manners
You are slumped over the table.	You chew with your mouth closed.
You eat with your fingers.	You wipe your mouth and hands with your napkin.
You talk with your mouth full.	You put your napkin on your knees.
You put your napkin on your head.	You use your fork, spoon, and knife to eat.
You wipe your hands on your pants.	You sit up straight.

Printed in November 2024 by Dimograf, Poland
Job number MGN 25L0038
Printed in compliance with the Consumer Protection
Safety Act, 2008